MOON MUSINGS

*Sacred activations
to soothe your soul*

ROMY WYSER

For you,

Remember who you are,
an eternal being filled with light,
divinely guided and
unconditionally loved.
May your path be blessed
and your soul enlightened as you
journey home to yourself.

———————

$\mathcal{P}$ROLOGUE

*We come spinning
out of nothingness,
scattering stars like dust.*

– RUMI –

—————

To write is to feel the layers of energy contained within every spark of thought, and witness it come alive from a place deep within that holds the innate mystery and cosmic dust from unexplainable origins. Each word written holds the resonance of the soul stories in this lifetime and beyond. These are my love letters to you. Gifted from experience and from the stars, inspired by the intimacy of heart-led conversations with soul seekers, dreamers, mystics and healers.

May these words carry seeds of hope and inspiration wherever you are on your soul journey.

Open your cosmic heart to the activations and the blessings, go deeper within the musings and you will discover answers and powerful reflections that reunite you with the sacred flame that burns brightly within.

You may choose to work with the wisdom of Moon Musings during your soul tending, for sacred Moon Rituals, celestial moments of stillness, and in divine synchronicity whenever the Universe wants to remind you of how blessed and loved you are.

It's a privilege to accompany you on your pathway for a little while as you come home to remember all that you are. And to lovingly remind you to leave your own legacy of light through the magical stories woven into your star-filled being.

Bright Blessings

Romy x

Contents

Earth Blessing

I'll bring you home each time you feel lost, light the hearth, and nourish your being so you feel my love for you.

My loyal presence will stand strong in winds of change and my branches will shelter you when you need respite from the storms.

I carry your story deep within my being and with every step you take upon Gaia's beating heart I will remind you of who you truly are.

You will feel my slow melodic drumming as I unfurl your tightly bound layers and awaken your cries to the wild, liberating you to tend to the seeds of hope within your heart as you journey into faraway lands that call you back to your roots.

I am the rich bounty that sustains your soul.

I nurture your roots with nature's song and share with you the enchantment and beauty of the wild.

I ground your restless heart and align you with the abundance that is rightly yours.

I remind you that you have everything you need and teach you how to find grace with all that you have.

I call to you through birdsong and the new beginnings of this season of growth.

I leave signs etched into ancient lands and call you forward to the places that feel familiar so you find where you truly belong.

My eruptions help you release your pain so that together we can plant new seeds of love that blossom into vibrant sanctuaries that soothe your soul.

Courage

My Courage is my Sacred Fire.

Courage backed me when they said it was too risky.

Courage held me when I had to face the unthinkable.

Courage searched for me when I'd lost my way.

Courage whispered to me when I was blinded from the truth.

Courage freed me when I was drowning in a heart full of regrets.

Courage inspired me when I couldn't see the way forward.

Courage protected me when connections had to be released.

Courage challenged me when I stopped showing up for myself.

Courage taught me which battles were worth fighting.

Courage honoured me when I struggled with the choices I had to make.

Courage stood beside me when I put my heart on the line.

Courage respected me when I surrendered to sacred rest.

Courage alchemised the aches over and over again.

Courage paved the way to forgiveness.

Courage believed in me when I struggled to feel I was enough.

Courage gathered me up when I broke, breathing fire back into the hollow space within.

Courage found me, wherever I was – an unwavering light devoting herself entirely to my path.

Courage taught me how to ask for what I needed and become unattached to all that I was seeking.

Courage demanded I be fearlessly proud to show up as me so I could follow my north star and feel peace within the belly of my soul.

Courage brought me faith and fortitude wrapped in endless life lessons and unshakeable love.

This is my Sacred Learning carved from the Sacred Wisdom that was shaped by my Sacred Experiences and gifted me my Sacred Certainty.

I trust in myself and in all the ways Courage will forever guide me to hold the light, be light, stand in the light, and shine the light.

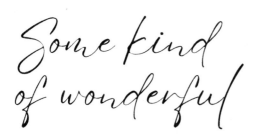

Some kind of wonderful

Something greater will always emerge from the strength I've shown.

Something beautiful will always grow where I've radiated the energy of love.

Something divine will always protect me when I need space to breathe.

Something magical will always guide me toward the answer my soul is ready to reveal.

Something extraordinary will always be ignited from my readiness to be brave.

Something to celebrate will always exist when I commit to my growth.

Something powerful will always unfold when I believe in better for myself.

Something healing will always replace what's been lost or broken.

Something joyful will always show up unexpectedly when I reconnect with myself.

Something inspiring will always drop in when I ask for the signs.

Some kind of wonderful is arriving for me today.

Wild Truths

I demand...

Truth that releases me.

Ideas that challenge me.

Love that expands me.

Desire that consumes me.

Opportunities that excite me.

Beliefs that liberate me.

My soul is restless, I've changed.

If you push me too far with untrained hands
I will shatter your delusions and return you
home to yourself.

You can't hide in wide-open planes or
capture this wild spirit.

I'm ready to leave it all behind.

So if you're joining me, then let old words
dissolve and lay old wounds to rest.

And show me something I've yet to see.

I create so I may honour my progress.

I love so I may open my heart to more,
forever seeking, shape-shifting through
the dark days but always finding the light.

I'm all in for the adventures that feel real.

Beginnings and endings are just a mirage.

All realities exist because I am infinite.

Everything falls away as I release
the illusion.

Standing on the edge of time and asking
for full disclosure.

Butterfly Kiss

The light splits in a kaleidoscope to reveal all possibilities exist.

The soul story reveals a new chapter as divine communication protects me in a place of serenity.

Changing minds and changing hearts lead to a deeper review of what's true.

That way of doing things simply doesn't work here anymore.

My butterfly soul now yearns for something not yet found, but felt in the fractions of light that cast colour into my world.

Here I'm already free.

Your rules may change but my fate is sealed.

Wonder, freedom, and love.

Peace, connection, and growth.

As my mind expands my spirit soars.

I've found my wings.

Earth Medicine and Magic

Earth medicine and magic cast their spells and fate steps in to direct the path.

The Moon walks the night silently dancing with a new destiny.

Held in-between worlds you open your heart to the stars and let out a breath that's been held for eternity.

This year may have stripped you of many things, but it couldn't take your fire, it hasn't taken your faith, and it will not steal your dreams.

When clouds collide and emotions rise up it's time for the chapter to close.

Your heart aches, yet bursts with anticipation.

Your soul yearns, yet feels more whole than it's ever felt.

Tethered to the past, yet flying free in new dimensions that radiate with light.

Worn out, weary and wistful, yet playing with possibility, fuelled by inspired awakening and the desire for more.

Retreating to soul search, whilst falling into infinite expansion.

Your thoughts flinch in doubt at the vastness of this climb, but silent whispers from within gather up your greatness and mirror it back to you.

Your heart merges with this mountain's protective wisdom.

Name this mountain faith and you will discover it.

Name this mountain strength and you will unearth it.

Name this mountain love and you will reveal it.

You are the pioneer of hope and each storm you summon, and that summons you clears the way for a deeper release and the divine deliverance of your dreams.

The Shattering

You shattered your peace to find something that felt real.

You shattered your mind to hear the truth over the lies.

You shattered your vision so growth could dawn a new light.

You shattered your heart and emerged from the wreckage.

It was here you discovered the pieces you'd abandoned, left strewn in gardens that have since grown wild.

And in the roaring silence of this unfamiliar place, gently you sat in the stillness, and tenderly you embraced them once more.

Untangling the vines to find the roots of a story older than time.

Your stability is rocked so you can build stronger foundations for the journey to come. Your faith is tested so you can develop a deeper certainty in your own value. Your boundaries are questioned so you can embody why you have them.

Love, tolerance, and growth will shine forth when you find the courage to break new ground in your own self-worth and you remain focused on the progress you have already made within yourself.

The delicate dance between your desires and your dreams and the grounded picture of a life that surrounds you, will coalesce delivering a potent and destiny-driven synchronicity to unlock the magic.

Starting Over

An invitation to begin anew...

When the noise finally grows quiet you will hear the sweet soul song of the birds and the heartbeat of the earth.

Peace will ascend from deep within the belly of your soul and in rhythm with the sun as it rises.

Here you will listen to the one true voice from within.

Here you will find the strength to begin again and the fire of faith will be lit within you, and you will light a thousand candles with that flame and they will light a thousand more, and so it will be, over and over until the waves of change have shown you that this was never a cage, but an invitation to step into your greatness.

An invitation to hold your wound gently like a child.

To nurture your aches thoughtfully and to listen to your fears curiously.

They each hold a gift and you will decipher their blessing with your heart open and your soul turned towards the light.

To be present and patient in this tug of war will illuminate that the only antidote is to be a warrior of love.

You are now the instigator of your own sacred flame.

With every grateful realisation.

With every powerful reflection.

With every solitary moment of peace.

You will rise, you will create, and you will prosper.

Your mind may feel frayed, but your heart will speak boldly.

You can build a new beginning out of nothing.

Anywhere at any time.

And your time is now.

Note to Self

There are still so many treasures to unearth.

A Renewed Spirit.

Purpose of Heart.

Celebration of the Climb.

Readiness to Let it Be.

Courage to Move on.

Respect for the Magic of being In-Between.

Forgiveness for the Tiredness.

Space to Tend to your Soul.

The Belief to say Yes.

The Bravery to say No.

Higher Conversations.

Dedication to Your Peace.

Nourishment for Your Mind.

Emotional Boundaries to allow time for
Sacred Rest.

Openness to Miracles.

Devotion to Loving Thoughts.

Receptivity to Growth.

The Richness of Time and the Presence
of Mindfulness to Appreciate it.

Hope

Hope wraps herself around sacred words entangling herself in conversation and deliberately showing up at the crossroads of change.

Hope isn't foolish or fearful.

She infuses light into narrow minds and seeds new growth into toxic lands.

Hope is stubborn and maverick, relentless in her deliverance of a soulful revolution.

She aligns herself with the cosmic shifts and evolving light language.

Breaking rules and forging bonds, she travels ethereally and works tirelessly.

Always right on time.

Hope is the wayshower, the wonder and the wisdom tucking herself deeply into your pockets grabbing your hand in the darkness and showering you with boundless courage.

She is defiant and determined.

Teaching you to live less afraid.

Open to the wide skies of possibility and promise.

Hope never gives up.

She's laying feathers in your path whilst placing swords of truth in your hands.

The peaceful warrior that never leaves your side.

Sacred Promises

I give myself permission to open to
new possibilities.

I give myself permission to change my mind,
my direction, and my muse.

I give myself permission to do things in my
own magically unique and moonstruck way.

I am willing to create new visions without
knowing how I will get there.

I am willing to communicate differently with
the desires that beat loudly in my heart.

I am willing to be misunderstood as I make
changes that better serve my soul.

May I receive the blessings of calmness, clarity, and wisdom to make choices that bring me joy.

May I dare to dream bigger, to demand more, and to question everything so as to discover what I now need to feel whole in my life.

May I see myself as worthy, capable and deserving of what I desire and free to seek even more.

I accept my restless mind and my wildly loving heart.

I accept there is no one thing that will satisfy the whole of me.

I accept my duality and my complexity for they help me to shapeshift through this colourful life.

I choose wonder, possibility, and love
I always choose love.

Crystalline Waters

You think you can't do it but you can.

You believe it's not possible but it is.

You feel it's too late but it's not.

You think you've not changed but you have.

You've swum through so many deep oceans, yet still, you feel the shore is out of sight, mythically holding the promise of home.

The inner struggle won't turn the tide.

So surrender here, into this sea of mystery.

And allow the energy shift direct you inwards.

A sanctuary that can't be destroyed or taken by the reckless chaos of the surface swell.

Dive deeper beneath the thoughts that trouble you, the hearts that confuse you, the circumstances that try to control you.

Beyond it all lies calm, crystal-clear waters.

Only once you let go of the frenzy and the fear will you find this sacred space for your soul to grow.

Where new visions emerge and ancient wisdom is found.

Time for You

Time to notice the details that bring the beauty of presence to your day.

Time to take care of yourself the way you do others.

Time to ground yourself to the earth and bring your healing heart to situations that will harmonise your world.

Time to keep something back that's just for you.

To use your energy wisely and tend to your passions wholeheartedly.

Time to discern what's really working and what truly isn't.

Time to breathe life back into what's been discarded or broken but intuitively is calling you back.

Time to set new rituals in place that support where you're going not where you've been.

Time to harness your power directly, to keep it real as you find solutions that deliver the tangible manifestations that are laced with your own unique blend of sacred wisdom.

Time to get more critical of the thought forms that aren't serving you and replace them with the language of love that you need to thrive.

Time for stillness to integrate all that's been learned and harvest all that's ready and ripe.

Time to shift gears to prepare for what's next. Observe the energy change and reorient your approach.

Time to nurture everything that matters with a whole new level of love and practical magic.

Dreamweaver

You unlock dreams and carry us on waves of inspiration till we reach the shore and discover the Jewell's of ancient myth and soul wisdom.

Your mutable energy shape shifts through experiences, finding layers of meaning in a world that others miss.

Your desire to feel everything splits your heart open over and over again. Your muse is awakened to celestial insights held in the stars. You gather them up and weave soulful stories that awaken minds and enlighten people to the treasures of this vast ocean of bounty waiting for us to dive into.

You flow through the days and search longingly through the nights. Waiting for things, sometimes things you don't understand, but you feel deep within your cosmic heart are waiting for you.

You bring lightness and divine knowing to the spaces you swim through. Leaving healing love notes of energy scattered for others to find in time.

You see the world through your own unique haze. Falling in and out of love and creating new sacred soul songs as you live each breath of the emotional journey in all dimensions and galaxies.

Star Child

Be patient with yourself sweet soul as a child of the stars, you will always shine brightest against the dark skies.

Place your hand on your heart feel its steady rhythm reminding you that you're here in this precious moment.

So be here where your spirit is radiant and your courage calls to you and home is a place that weaves light deep within your soul.

Vision Quest

I am not one grain of sand, I am the whole desert.

I do not shine as one star I am the entire galaxy.

My roots do not connect to one tree; they breathe life into all living things.

To see me now you must acknowledge the whole of me.

My Earth Medicine soothes your soul and whispers wise words laced with coloured ribbons of love.

But only step forward if you're ready to journey all the way with me.

I'm working in harmony with myself and I won't be swayed.

Weaving the integration of my lessons deep into the layers of my frayed heart.

I breathe out the impatience and settle into graceful acceptance.

I am the bridge between worlds as I tend seeds into the rich earth and draw in light from the angels to watch them burst into life.

I'm taking steps in faith to transform my world observing every detail unfold in gratitude.

Ready for conversations that will strip away the falseness and reveal the beauty that lies at the heart of this stillness amidst the storms.

I am crafting a new space in my life, where there are no lines to fit inside or rules to abide by.

My Vision Quest is calling me, my heart is leading me.

This is how I rise.

Unshakeable

You're unshakable when you remember...

Nothing can take your essence, your soul.

Nothing can strip you of the lifetime of experiences that shaped and carved you from the grit and the ache that you spun and alchemised into the gift of your wisdom.

Nothing can take the memories that brought light to the moments that you cherish.

Nothing can steal your ability to dream new visions and be moved to new inspiration.

Nothing can stop your stubborn heart from believing, embracing and trusting the infinite ways the Universe shows you how worthy you are.

Nothing can change the way you feel about watching the sunrise and seeing the stars emerge in a clear night sky.

Nothing will prevent you from what your spirit knows is your journey for this lifetime, the battle scars and the triumphs, the courage and the craziness.

Nothing can stop the unconditional love that your Higher Self wraps you in each and every day.

Nothing can take your freedom to choose one kind and loving thought after another as you align with the unshakable peace in the sanctuary of your soul.

Perfectly Flawed

I am perfectly flawed.

I tried to tame this wild heart but its voice just got louder demanding to colour outside the lines, so I listened.

I am crafting a new space in my life, where there are no rules, learning how to hold on and how to let go, and show up just as I am, perfectly flawed.

I tried your way and your way didn't work for me.

I can't be all those things you want me to be.

Don't place me on your pedestal and try to hold me back or you won't see the beauty of my rise.

I can't fit into those boxes and walk those straight lines.

My spirit is unleashed, I need to breathe different air now.

So I will do this my way.

I will stumble and I will fall and I will rise each and every time.

I will lose pieces of myself along the way, and then I will meet them again as I rest a while and let the earth deliver its healing hands deep into my bones.

I will find a rhythm with this that makes sense only to me.

I need no validation.

I require no permission.

I am an apprentice only to my own self-mastery.

I trust only the light that illuminates within and sends endless messages to guide me forward.

I invest in my ability to figure it out.

I am creating my path brick by brick.

I cannot do this for you or for them.

I do it to find my peace, my connection.

To colour outside of my lines.

Here is where the vortex of boundless grace finds me.

Here is where my heart blossoms and my soul sings.

Silver Threads

There's a better way.

Sitting in skies of hope, cradled by grace,
I challenge myself to see something new.

Silver threads hang from stars, each one
offers a new possibility to play with.

Confusion reigns but silence speaks.

To know their secrets, I must give up mine.

Pulled towards a future that wants to
be rewritten.

Challenged to change.

It's not who I am that holds me back, it's all
that I believe I'm not.

I welcome the wholeness within, and let go
in the surrender of the exhale.

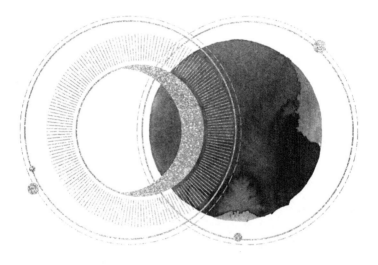

Portals of Possibility

Expect *greatness* and it will wrap around you in radiant golden hues.

Invite *stillness* and it will greet you with honesty at the edge of your quietness.

Embrace *light* and it will connect you to a consciousness that transcends this dimension.

The ecstasy and the ache of your growth deliver a powerful charge to your cosmic heart.

In the heavenly light of the Spiritual Sun, your time to evolve is now.

The energy breathes new light and illuminates change bringing a cathartic and cleansing pause to assimilate and attract.

You may need to wade through some haze before you discover the crystal-clear visions you seek.

Soothe your soul as you meet any uncomfortable emotions and keep letting yourself move into the growth of this season.

Reflections are deep and heartfelt. Tap into your cosmic heart to feel this power.

Material manifestations are charged, manage your mind and your thoughts to keep them wrapped in gold.

Keeper of
the Stars

You're the keeper of the stars, guiding us through the cycles so that we shine through them all.

You invite us to place our hand on our heart feeling its steady rhythm reminding us that we are here in this precious moment.

So let us be here where our spirit is radiant and our courage shines and home is a place that weaves light deep within our soul.

You show us how to surrender to the winds of fate and embrace our destiny knowing we are always free.

You bring lightness to the heaviness we hold and pour liquid gold on our ideas so they explode in colour and richness beyond our wildest imagination.

Inviting us to rise on the cosmic waves of light and sound, you teach us to embrace our duality, to express our words with truth as you wrap them in divine white light.

You're a heart-filled gift falling from the sky. Strength wrapped in clouds that shower light-filled feathers that help us find our wings to fly as many times as it takes.

You're the butterfly that comes to light the way. The angel of the winds that clears the path. You remind us that our restless soul will always be searching for more and that our stories must be honoured and shared.

Mutable and shape-shifting you're here to hold us through the many transitions as you remind us of the future visions we're aligning with, and the destiny that's written in the energy we're meeting with open eyes, curious minds and sensitive hearts.

Reflections

Show me what you fear most and I will reveal to you the bravery that carried you to this place.

And how you've become more because of it.

Share your sorrow and I will mirror your strength back to you so that you remember how you've survived despite your aching loss.

And how you've become more because of it.

Confide in me the doubts that kept you restless in the dark and I will send waves of light that lift you beyond your struggles.

And you will become more child of the stars.

The Unravelling

My soul no longer fits inside of this life I've created.

I need more.

I am more.

I've moved beyond that mountain you placed before me and I no longer fear the terrain.

Everything unravelled on that climb, pieces of me died and I wondered why you pushed me so far.

But the medicine of my wild and free spirit brought growth from the grit and expansion from the exhaustion.

And now I stand on this summit reflecting on how I came alive in the chaos and mystery of it all.

I look towards the horizon and embrace endless new possibilities.

I have fire breathing life inside of these tired bones and I will not be tamed.

So talk to me of leading-edge truths that take me beyond these limitations, so I can shatter the illusions I still cling to.

Show me the adventures yet to come and let hope flood into the spaces I've created for it.

I will listen without judgement and own the story you mirror back to me of this one daring and brave life I'm living.

Where every loss has become my greatest victory and every wound my battle scar of truth.

Now I see a new quest emerging and it rings loudly in my ears and beats strongly in my heart.

There is no way back.

So I will welcome in the wide-open plains that hold the endless belief of a better way, a better life, and a better me.

The Light of Possibility

I don't live in the darkness of my doubts but in the light of possibility.

There's fire within me.

I make no apology for it.

Tell me there's no path and I'll clear a way through.

Try to say I should give up and I will go further than you thought possible.

I'll fight harder and I will shine brighter.

I own my fire.

I own it when it burns everything to ashes.

I own it when it breathes everything back to life.

Charging me with the strength to start over as many times as it takes.

I AM fearless and I AM ready.

I listen to the energy that speaks of courage, taking chances and changing rhythms.

I command this power, and it calls up a fire dragon within me.

I feed it the truth and in turn, it sparks my brave and devours my doubt so I walk in the light of possibility.

Dreamer, Mystic, Healer

I am the dreamer, the mystic and the healer. My heart is as deep as the ocean, flooding your senses to wash away clouds of doubt and soothe the fiery wounds that catch in your throat.

I show you how to listen as the sea sings to you with ancient wisdom and delivers magic from her watery depths. I guide you in whispering rhythmic waves of light and sound. Into the blue, you will find comfort in my embrace.

I teach you to trust your empathic soul and remember your true purpose. My knowing helps you to navigate your way through the turbulent rivers as they carve their way through new lands and reveal glistening opportunities for you to discover.

I create peaceful lakes to ease your troubled mind and I nourish your roots, breathing life into your beautiful soul so that you may blossom into the Goddess of light that you are.

My eternal love for you will shine through the moonlight and reflect back to you the exquisite perfection of your intricate layers, reminding you to surrender to the universal stream that flows to you with never-ending gifts, grace and abundance and your worthiness to receive it.

You Broke

You broke...

You broke your own limits to reach for something more.

You broke your own heart so you could feel the beauty of everything.

You broke through the lies to silence the noise.

You broke through the fear to fight for your peace.

You broke the darkness and flooded it with light.

You broke their expectations so you could feel freer.

You broke down the barriers and exposed the truth.

You broke the stillness to reveal its secrets.

And when it was all laid bare and nothing and no one could hide, you asked for more.

And then the Moon called you out from the shadows and you stood beneath a canopy of stars and you felt your peace.

Wild truth seeped from your brave soul and your untamed heart.

Deep desire and lifelong craving unleashed.

You rose from the chaos.

You rose from the ashes.

You rose from the fragments of a life you thought had been certain.

And then the earth wept as your rebirth flooded everything with love and you remembered who you were.

The Butterfly and The Phoenix

Love always finds me when I'm in the beauty of transition.

Like the Butterfly, I find my wings.

Like the Phoenix, I rise from the ashes.

My wisdom is deep and my courage is strong.

Infinite new possibilities abound and I value myself enough to say yes to the life I want.

I know endings and beginnings will merge and through it all, I will become more.

I am healing and feeling the shift as I evolve into a deeper radiance and readiness for growth.

The fire breathes new life into my desires and I bravely seize the moment.

I'm making every day count and it will reward me with infinite blessings.

Let it Happen

Let it happen.

The leaves fall from the trees when they're ready to let go.

The raindrops fall when the clouds become too heavy to hold them.

The sun sets when it's time for it to kiss the day goodbye.

Allow the changes in your life to flow without resistance.

Let it happen.

New foundations are forming.

Heightened sensitivity is emerging.

Beautiful breakthroughs are arriving.

Revelations for your highest good are dawning.

Energetic alignment with what you desire is unfolding.

Allow your mind to be soothed and your heart awakened to this portal of release, wisdom and expansion.

Let it happen.

Cracking Open

Infinite possibilities abound.

My shell has been cracked open and my senses are awakened to a new chorus of light.

The rhythm here is softer and it soothes my sensitive soul.

I choose to feel my way into this radiant vortex of hope leaving behind old words and constrained hearts.

Stripped back by the waves, I align to my own tenderness.

A new dawn of promise has secrets to share.

Some come crashing in on wild rapids and some cast barely a ripple on the clear waters of truth.

This is a sacred space I now hold.

For me and for you.

I wait, poised for the reveal.

Watching as the dance between the light and the shadow
plays out.

I force nothing, destiny is already in motion.

I've listened to these symphonies before and this time
I know to root deeper into the earth as the energies rise.

Comfort exists in these changing tides for I know they
unearth greater gifts that allow softness to flow and
strength to rise up.

Nothing is good or bad in this space. It simply "is".

There will be no struggle here as I choose to vibrate higher
and my soul sings in triumph of the love that abounds in
the infinite possibility of it all.

A Maverick Heart

When it looked like there was nowhere left to turn,
I looked inside myself.

I challenged everything.

And you challenged me.

I refused to accept what no longer harmonized with my heart.

They thought I'd lost my mind but really, I'd just found my soul.

I watched as fate stepped in, she unlocked the gilded cage and suddenly I felt free.

A Maverick soul with a heart that runs wild.

It was always my story.

I don't need you to understand me.

I don't need you to validate me.

I am the innovator of my own journey and I embrace the expansion of this as I uproot myself over and over again.

I don't have to prove my worthiness to feel the benevolence of Source.

I let go of the game of control you wanted to play.

I gravitate only towards that which stretches my mind and brings in better.

Better energy.

Better terms.

Better choices.

A better me.

I seek love where it flows without condition, I meet it with a heart so full it magnetises a future of illuminated understanding and deeper connection.

Here is where my story really begins.

Courage comes alive in the surrender to your sacred knowing.

Do you even know the greatness of your soul? I'll never stop showing you.

Watch me rise.

Enlightened in the Exhale

Breathe into the beauty

Breathe into the revelations

Breathe into the wound

Breathe into the truth

Breathe into the light and the shadow

Breathe into the loss

Breathe into the release

Breathe into the struggle

Breathe into the joy

Breathe into the ache

Breathe into the love

Breathe into the separation

Breathe into the connection

Breathe into the chaos and the calm

Breathe into your power

You are loved and all is well.

Waves Crash and Stars Fall

When your waves are crashing and your stars are falling you're still worthy, loved and infinitely deserving of all that you seek.

Your medicine lies within your own sacred energy.

Let no one and nothing disrupt this knowing.

The wisdom of your soul will always be your true north guide, carrying you home to where peace reigns and stillness sighs in a loving welcome at the sight of your arrival.

I'm so proud of you, in awe of your strength, and your readiness to weather the storms, so go easy today and soothe your soul to nourish that beautiful heart of yours.

It deserves your tenderness and your presence.

You're ok, be all in with this truth and you'll find your way back, moment by moment, breath by breath.

Love Letters from Heaven

I walk with the sun and the moon and the stars and together we create a new kind of magic, weaving soul stories that open portals of change and transport me to places where all I see is the golden light of possibility, love and joy. I am more than I've ever been and it's only the beginning of me allowing the abundance of well-being that's flowing into my pathway to peace.

Here my radiant heart is held with the grace of an army of angels and my soul is filled with the light of rainbow rays and destined dreams. As I stand beneath their healing hues all I feel is the sweet relief of coming home to myself and the miracle of opening to a life that's been patiently waiting for me to receive it.

I'm ready to run wildly into a journey of adventure and bliss, and I do it all with your love protectively watching over me, littering my path with beautiful signposts of your devoted presence and the gift of your heavenly kiss.

I am so blessed.

Alchemy

Angry > Show Love

Frustrated > Embrace Love

Disillusioned > Seek Love

Helpless > Speak Love

Fearful > Become Love

Uncertain > Allow Love

You'll Find a Way

You'll find a way…

You'll find a reason to keep swimming against the current.

You'll find faith when you thought the well had run dry.

You'll find new friendships on the journey to a new life.

You'll find a deeper respect for yourself as you make the tough decisions.

You'll find yourself after the storm clears and you'll embrace the beauty of what you see.

You'll find love in the unexpected.

You'll find love in the chaos.

You'll find love in the loneliness.

You'll find love everywhere your heart stays defiant and open.

You'll find treasure in the dirt and see its value, and yours.

You'll find the answers to soothe you during the sleepless nights.

You'll find a way to move on or to make your way back.

This time in readiness for more.

You'll find the strength.

You'll find the resolve.

You'll find the belief.

You'll find stillness in the exhale.

You'll find light in the whispers that affirm *keep going.*

You'll find your way.

Soothe your Soul

Nurture your body

Nourish your mind

Tend to your soul

Release your struggles

Forgive your disappointments

Heal your heart

Honour your growth

Bless the earth

Accept your truth

Reveal your strength

Receive new wisdom

Listen to your thoughts

Change your thoughts

Watch your breath

Exhale the stress

Make your wishes

Devote to your cause

Cleanse your space

Love where you've been

Love where you are

Love the distance to where you want to be

Love yourself

Love yourself

Love yourself

The Ecstasy and The Ache

A heart built to survive because it broke a thousand times.

Courage born from a spirit that never gave up.

A path of slow growth that planted deep roots.

A soul strengthened by the awakening and ready to rise.

When the storm surge rose up, you were the ocean.

When the tides turned, you became the wind.

When the waves crashed, you embraced the silence that followed.

You honoured the river of your own healing, flowing towards an expanding horizon of possibility.

Searching for where the light poured in.

Integrating the stories that came from tired days and wistful nights.

Now ready for the exhale.

The ecstasy and the ache of it levelled you. It led you deeper into the abyss before drenching you in love and returning you home to yourself forever changed.

Celebrate all the richness this journey gifted to you. Holding a celestial space whilst you let the beauty of it dance through your soul and imprint in your heart.

Your courage only got stronger; your spirit only got brighter. Your goodbye may be bittersweet but the new path is calling you and it's flooded with radiant light.

There's no room for regrets only wisdom born from fearless experience. Wisdom is now entwined in your life force and shaping your tomorrows with reverence and grace.

Storm Chaser

I know you want me to stay in the shallows, but there's nothing real there for me anymore.

I want depth, devotion and undeniable truth.

I see light in the shadows, where others are spellbound.

I can't stay in a life where there's nowhere to breathe.

I've endured a thousand mini deaths to meet this moment.

Each time rising stronger in belief and softer in sacred trust.

It's all or nothing now.

Awakened in a world whose heart is split open by reckless hands.

But whose healing emerges from enlightened words.

Storms still run wild in the hidden corners of my soul.

Birthing new stars to fill the hollow void of loss.

Deep promises made in the dark now blooming wild and burning brightly.

Deep faith found in the unknown lighting the way for boundless grace.

Nothing will change until I do.

And in my readiness to receive I'm changing everything.

Sacred Trust

I'm all things in this liminal space.

With quiet thoughts but unravelling desires.

Subdued and reflective, but awakened
and fearless.

Untamed and wild, yet tethered to the
presence of peace I've nurtured for myself.

I'm listening now trusting myself more
fervently, learning how to be mine, feeling
my energy without the drain of those who
kept taking when there was nothing left
to give.

Revelling in the purity of how it feels to
come home to myself.

I'm the dreamer and the healer.

Remembering all the moments when life
rescued me until I discovered how to
rescue myself.

Feeling into this new space with soulful
surrender.

Levelled by the journey.

Sitting with the earth, letting it all go,
letting it all in.

The Pilgrimage

A soul call.

Trying to be ready to be ready.

Without the promise of where it leads.

The honesty of grief carves the way.

Letting go of all that you knew so you're open to discovering all the secrets that you didn't know.

Moving with a new energy that feels awkward and unfamiliar but vital and alive.

All that was hidden within now becoming your greatest gift to give.

New horizons birthed from courageous conversation.

Exiled but finally home.

Celestial Stillness

You had a vision of how life would be.

But it changed suddenly and without your permission.

A momentary shift that changed everything.

Beneath the turmoil and the chaos, lighter vibrations were emerging.

You felt them rising up.

They brought stillness, so you listened.

They invited surrender, so you released.

They brought tenderness, so you embraced.

They brought peace, so you accepted.

A new conversation revealed itself.

You're so much further than you know.

You're a miracle of recovery, endurance and faith.

Your immeasurable value illuminated in a life full of fracture lines that are healed but still felt.

A mind full of excitement but still cautious with fear.

A heart that beats loyally to the love that you hold.

And a soul whose soil is too rich not to bloom.

So rest easy my love as the Moon soothes your soul.

Step by step, thought by thought, breath by breath.

See the worthiness in all that you are, so that you may cease walking with the heaviness of your doubt and flow into the lightness of your trust.

Only then will you observe the pieces knit together in magical new ways that reveal to you, You're so much further than you know...

Queen of Light

My strength rises from the rejection I've faced.

It burns brightly from the failures I've overcome, and it carries me beyond the troubles I've endured.

My fire burns clean.

A sacred violet flame that turns wounds into wisdom.

So I won't be limited by these scarcity thoughts or suppressed by your beguiling words.

You can't break what drives me because it's not of this world.

Faith is my fuel and it blazes through me like wildfire.

I know the tale of breaking open.

My journey is etched with scars from the battles I've won and lost.

You can't tame me.

I'm a soul created from thousands of stories, each one held in the stars that unwaveringly guide me forward.

I'm letting it go, the illusion you cast.

I'm under my own reign now.

The Queen of my own light.

Breaking the Spell

They'll disappoint you and you'll respect yourself more determinedly.

They'll provoke you and you'll nurture yourself more tenderly.

They'll attempt to break you and you'll forgive yourself more deeply.

They'll try to deceive you and you'll embody the truth more emphatically.

They'll try to control you and you'll free yourself more powerfully.

They'll take from you and you'll gift others even more generously.

They'll withhold from you and you'll love yourself more unconditionally.

They'll try to silence you and you'll speak more defiantly.

They'll try to imitate you and you'll evolve more uniquely.

You must breathe in the stillness when the world shakes around you.

It's a love affair of divinity and darkness.

Endless circles that bring you home to a new legacy of light.

The spell of words cast power in your path.

See through them, move beyond them, rise above them.

Stand guard at the gates of your mind so your sacred self may flourish.

But soften your heart so you remain open to receive all that is destined for you.

Become the matrix and you will thrive.

Fierce Love

This is how I'll grow...

With *Fierce Love* to drown out the hate.

With *Deep Roots* to build something real from my visions.

With *Raw Courage* to say what my heart needs to express.

With *Brave Choices* to face fear and rise strong.

With *Protective Wings* that carry me beyond the struggle.

With *Daring Moves* that demonstrate how much I believe in me.

With *Endless Hope* to ignite even the darkest days.

With *Determined Honesty* to strip away the shallow and draining connections.

With *Roaring Passion* to awaken the muse.

With a *Wild Heart* to invite in energies that spark my flame.

With *Loyal Intentions* that serve my soul.

I've Got You

When the solar storms overwhelm you, It's in the stillness you find your breath, where your struggle becomes your strength.

When the void consumes you, It's in the calmness you feel your truth, where hope gathers in secret places.

When the heaviness obscures the path, It's in the quietness your vision gets clear, and your soul softens to allow it.

When the tiredness wrecks you, It's in the restfulness your body awakens, as you soothe it with nature's nourishment.

When the divide devastates you, It's in the sacred you find the answers, a voyage of soul retrieval to remember who you are.

When the doubts crush you, It's in the serenity you find your peace, where oceans of love heal the shipwrecks in your soul.

When you have no words, the stars will speak your language.

When you have no faith, the healing rivers will carry you.

When you have no answers, the divine light will find you.

When you don't know if you're ok.

Your higher self is whispering *I've got you.*

Child of the Sun

Listen closely child of the sun the universe is daring you.

Daring you to find deeper meaning in your life and act on it.

Daring you to express yourself in beautiful, bold expressions of light.

Daring you to start over and let sunshine fill your soul where wounds split you open.

Daring you to put your heart on the line.

Daring you to surrender to what has been taken.

Daring you to colour in the voids with radiant hues of divine love.

Daring you to crown yourself worthy of a life that lifts you higher.

Daring you to drink in the Moonlight and choose aliveness over despair.

Daring you to ask your heart daily what it needs to thrive and choosing that path over and over until you feel the greatness of a galaxy being illuminated within you.

No more lip service, your soul is calling you up.

Signs are falling from heaven with your name embellished in gold.

Open your heart and find your fire.

This is your time to create something, unlike anything you have known before.

Compelled to share your authentic fire you will seek to be heard for the truth of what burns in your heart.

You are harmonizing your world and the universe will reflect your acts of valour with a bounty of blessings.

Have faith and courage that the constellations are guiding you unwaveringly toward what is destined for you.

Time Traveller

I don't want convention.

I want the freedom to be me.

I'm earthbound, but I play amongst the stars.

A time traveller to these sacred lands.

I won't check out.

I'm in this now.

All in, and all the way.

It's a tsunami of love and it can't be stopped.

So show me silver linings and we'll figure it out.

I'll be heroic when things keep crumbling.

Casting out a constellation of new visions for you to anchor into.

The audacity to give a sacred no will be my right.

The certainty to commit to a soulful yes will be my guide.

I can't live half-alive with those half-awake
pretending with their half-hearted words.

Can't you see?

I'm hungry for the truth.

Starving for realness.

Yearning for nourishment.

So I'm leaning all the way in.

A mind full of possibility and promise.

A heart full of faith.

Everything can feel hard under this tension.

Until you decide it's not.

I'll meet you in that space.

For it's full of wonder and wisdom and the
exquisite beauty of miracles dancing in the
breeze and waiting to be felt.

Doorways to Dreams

You see the old ways crumbling and the new energy powering forth.

You see dreams shaping a new future directed with arrows of light and possibility.

You see the quest emerging, bright and vibrant on the horizon.

The light of truth collides with the dissonance of reality.

A new light language must be expressed to navigate the tidal shift of this collision.

The future no longer a mirror of the past but a limitless galaxy of opportunity.

You watch as the broken pieces melt in the fire, a molten mess shapeshifting into something beautiful, poetic and beyond expectation.

You are the energy expression of endless endings and new beginnings.

Standing in the doorways to your dreams, lighting up the dark nights with visions of possibility and promise.

You cannot be caged for your mind is always free and your soul strengthened by truth and now laced together with unwavering fire and faith.

Aura

I'm here to quiet your fear and announce your brilliance.

I'm here to lift you up when the meaning of it all got lost in the wind.

I'm here to prepare you for all that you've yet to do by challenging you to overcome all that you think you're not.

I'm here to soothe you, to enlighten you, and to gift you rapturous moments strung together with love that never fades or falters.

I'm here to release the sunshine and direct the moonlight into your heart so you keep seeing yourself in the light of your true essence.

I'm here to praise you unconditionally when you momentarily forget the magic of all that you are.

I'm here, endlessly weaving light within your celestial field of radiant colour.

Full Moon Blessing

I feel deeply into the quiet space that whispers the secrets of how I am rising like the Phoenix, transforming my life into something epic and empowered.

My trust is anchored in newfound self-respect and belief.

Knitted together with promise and possibilities.

I am awakening to the truth of how aligned I am now with all that I desire.

This moment is beautiful and I let my inner fire burn brightly.

It breathes life back into all that is ready to come alive and I feel this energy surge through my whole being.

I know the layers I'm releasing are creating space for the greatest adventures I've yet to experience in my life.

I trust the map of my soul as it guides me deeper into the mysteries of the universe and my beautiful journey within it.

I receive the healing energies and dive soulfully into a newfound self-belief that will carry me far beyond this place. Here my heart will soar at the sight of what is being revealed on the horizon.

I no longer accept "just enough" everything in my life now overflows with abundant blessings, wisdom and joy.

Sacred Full Moon Release

I release the weight of your expectations.

I release the discomfort of feeling stuck, lost, less than and powerless.

I release the comfort, that's really the pattern, that's really the self-sabotage that comes from the fear that emerges when I declare I'm ready for change.

I release the hurtful, toxic and wounded words I've absorbed externally; I've thought internally and I've expressed in disconnection from myself.

I release any projection from energies that make me feel scared, wrong, confused, shameful or guilty.

I release the need to be what "you" need me to be, or who "I think" I need to be, to feel accepted.

I only need to embrace all that I am in this moment.

I release the stories of struggle, scarcity and selling out on my real value.

I release the beliefs that limit me, the cords that drain me, and the burdens that distract me from nourishing myself, so I may live in balance, peace and joy.

I welcome oceans of blessings as I voyage towards a life where I'm in complete harmony with myself and the earth.

I welcome beautiful, conscious relationships that are earth medicine to my evolving, complex and deeply loving soul.

I welcome deliberate, intentional and empowered decisions that keep me curious, alive, free and in a sacred union of complete trust with myself.

I welcome who I've become. I celebrate the journey and all it's taken to meet her here in this extraordinary moment.

I welcome the surrender of letting it go, knowing my infinite capacity to heal, transform and rise in higher waves of love, wisdom and strength.

New Moon Blessing

I give permission for all my relationships to evolve at this time leading me to greater awareness and acceptance of their role in my journey.

I release the heaviness of worn-out stories. My thoughts are of adventures and conversations that spark revolutions.

I am the author of my life. I choose my words and wishes with deliberate intent. Watching as they echo into my future, laying a golden path to guide me toward my desires and my destiny.

I release the ache of disappointment and the pain of staying stuck whilst tending to the wounds that need my loving prayers.

With the space this creates I play with wonder and curiosity. I celebrate the wisdom of knowing better and the courage I have birthed to embrace the change.

A sense of devotion to this enlightened version of myself brings me home with the knowing that I am becoming more secure in who I am with every day that passes.

There is nothing that holds me back from accessing the magnificent depths of this wise vessel of power and peace within me.

I am capable, worthy, resilient and constantly evolving into a more liberated and awakened soul.

I am whole and I release anything that dares to limit this truth.

New Moon Sacred Ceremony

May your courage be reclaimed.

May your heart be expressed.

May your soul be rejuvenated.

May your belief be strengthened.

May your struggle be supported.

May your energy be charged.

May your mind be opened.

May your choices be bountiful.

May your decisions be wise.

May your love be wild and spirited.

May your loneliness be comforted.

May your abundance be overflowing.

May your pain be soothed.

May your journey be celebrated.

The New Moon cycle is a fusion of potent energy that will be for you what you choose to make of it. Not just words to read, but emotions to be felt, desires to be ignited and intentions to be set. We become that which we embody and your greatest role is to now live the teachings you have absorbed, so you may evolve to new levels of consciousness.

May you dedicate this day and every one after this towards the greatness that is within you. The opportunities that surround you. The survivals that are behind you and the lightness that lies ahead of you.

Where is your fire?

No matter if it's just a flicker, a roaring flame or a wild blaze. It's what nourishes your brave and powers your faith.

Let it breathe.

Miracles happen when we accept that they do.

Let your heart roar loudly and believe to receive the energy activation of something magical.

You are destiny unfolding in real-time.

You are energy transforming and a soul evolving.

You're everything you've ever wanted to be.

But the truth is...

You're so much more than that.

Gaia's Blessing

I am at one with the seasons and the cycles of life.

I devote myself to nurturing and sustaining my light so I may bring generosity of spirit and fertile richness to all that I align with.

I radiate a loving expression of infinite abundance that waters the roots of everything in my world calling into bloom all that is ready to be received.

I soothe the mother wound within me leading you to mirror this healing within you, so we may rise in peace and acceptance of the divine energy calling us into greatness.

My soul is ready to allow transformative energy to the connections that strengthen or release their presence in my life.

I sit in peace and harmony, grateful for the gift of Gaia's loving presence, patience and powerful protection, as I seek to meet her deepest knowing and her eternal vision for alchemising the ache of mindless neglect.

Equinox Blessing

I make peace with the shadow

I make peace with the uncertainty

I make peace with letting go

I make peace with the changes

I make peace with my knowing

I make peace with the revelations

I make peace with my unresolved feelings

I make peace with my truth

I reclaim my body

I reclaim my dreams

I reclaim my choices

I reclaim my love

I reclaim my power

I reclaim my voice

I reclaim my peace

I reclaim my energy

I reclaim my time

I reclaim my worthiness

Embrace a new point of stillness in mind, breath, body and soul. It's a sacred day to reflect upon the internal shifts you've experienced and heralds a time of renewal, reset and rebirth.

The cosmic shift you'll feel is inevitable, it may disrupt your equilibrium initially as it performs a powerful clearing before bringing you back home to yourself with an entirely new perspective. Go gently but purposely into this beautiful energetic exchange. The way you choose to express yourself and how you're interpreting the steady stream of information you are absorbing will be levelled. Enlightened choices that reflect both the duality and the oneness that exists within you will emerge.

This powerful celebration should be understood from a place of deep acceptance in the cycles of change so you can witness the miracles of the divine order of everything.

Solstice Blessing

May a cloak of stillness serenade your soft and searching heart.

May the fading light make way for a perpetual sunrise in your soul.

May you be nourished by the silence of the earths slow retreat into peaceful slumber.

May eternal echoes of your ancestors protect your deepest knowing.

May you bathe in the golden glowing embers of the year's final bow to celestial ceremony.

May sacred gifts woven through streams of starlight entangle themselves in the destiny of your dreams.

May the midnight spectacle of shooting stars alchemise layers of doubt as their parting kiss of cosmic dust and magic foretells of your greatest days yet to come.

May you dance in-between time as all that is unlived within you becomes lovingly claimed and gracefully blessed, until the sacredness of your vow unfolds with heavenly intervention.

May you witness divine consciousness birth brilliance through your eternal cosmic heart as you transition into a new cycle of presence and power.

May the memories of the year land softly to stir you from your sleep, enlightened in the beauty of the exhale as you receive new secrets, they're now ready to share.

May you surrender to the passing of this year in celebration of your devoted journey. Courageously gathering up the pieces both broken and beautiful as you bless your weary, wistful and wondrous voyage.

May the sanctuary of darkness offer a void where no thoughts trouble you and the angels lull you in their celestial embrace.

May you stumble joyously into love in all its rich colour and sweet sounds and vibrant energy enveloping you in belonging and gifting you golden treasures for your soul.

May you come home to yourself.

May you appreciate yourself.

May you make peace with yourself.

As you celebrate Solstice and the slowing down for a sacred pause to honour the dance between light and dark, may you align with the radiance of your own soul as you release old energies and come into harmony with the changing rhythm of the earth's whispers.

A portal of powerful change and seasonal alignment. Witness the celestial stillness as you reconnect and rebalance your world, feeling into your closest relationships and your creative expression, seeking to unify your vision to one of peace and receptivity to all that is ready to emerge as you release and celebrate this sacred time.

An Ocean Blessing

May you move like water carving a way through even the most challenging of paths.

Allowing your emotions to rise and fall with grace and acceptance.

May you find moments of stillness, calm and serenity then effortlessly become a powerful revolutionary wave of change.

May you feel nourished and cleansed so that you water your whole life with love.

May you never sacrifice your depth and your mystery, yet still find joy and playfulness in your childlike spirit.

May you be soothed by the sounds of waves breaking, rain falling, waterfalls cascading and rivers flowing.

May you find peace within the oceans of your soul.

A Blessing for Divine Destiny

May you be held protectively as the world shakes around you.

May you release the darkness of your doubts and nestle into the light of your worthiness.

May you embrace the challenging revelations without losing your trust in the destiny of your path.

May you illuminate the burdens so you can clearly see what you're ready to release in an honest soulful surrender.

May you deliberately choose to embrace all that is loving and courageous and radically hopeful, even in the ruins that appear to offer no respite for your tired splintered soul.

May you mindfully remember it takes only one moment to change your thoughts, your reaction and your energy.

And that time is now.

May you step into your greatness and it feels like you're finally home.

May you say yes to yourself in all the ways your heart is waiting for you to allow.

May you above all else remember your value is never wrapped up in the opinion of others, but in the exquisite life experiences that have shaped you, where you've refused to give up, and you've continued to find your way back to the treasures of your beautiful sacred soul.

A Blessing for your Worthiness

My mind, body and spirit flourish when I allow myself
to unlock the wisdom of my deepest inner knowing.

This harmonizing energy is the inner well that I will
nourish with every breath of presence and peace.

I seek balance within so I may move in peace and purpose
in the connections that greet me, the love that seeks me
and the pathways that challenge me to become more.

My inner compass guides me to forever stay true
to myself in loving respect, deep compassion and
eternal worthiness.

My home is a sacred place that exists within my heart.
Here I am safe. Safe to open up to the secrets of time, the
wonders of the universe, and the certainty of trusting
myself wholly and completely in a vortex of love.

There is nothing that holds me back from accessing
the depths of this wise and magnificent vessel of power
and peace.

I am capable, worthy, resilient and constantly evolving to
higher vibrations of light.

A Blessing for Trust

When the pull of something magical hits a wall of doubt, *I will move deeply into trust and let lightness fill my soul.*

When the challenges that lay before me feel greater than my bravery, *I will move deeply into trust and let lightness fill my soul.*

When the chaos of what is spoken is at odds with what I feel inside my heart, *I will move deeply into trust and let lightness fill my soul.*

When I'm provoked to align with a disjointed version of the truth, I will remember the certainty of my sacred inner knowing and *I will move deeply into trust and let lightness fill my soul.*

A Blessing for Freedom

I claim my wholeness today and release anything that denies me this reality.

I see new patterns emerging in the way I think. Thoughts are becoming less tangled with the past, free to roam and explore what's next without limit or expectation. I meet this moment with curiosity and calm as I discover who I'm becoming and receive the gifts of this bounty.

I direct my energy to what serves to expand the goodness in my life. Kindness and love are showered onto my path as I lift myself beyond the heaviness of doubt and into the sacred certainty of trust within myself.

I'm awakened to the true beauty within me and it's changing everything.

I'm emerging from any struggles with the strength, courage and wisdom to initiate change and allow for my expansion into greatness, gratitude and peace.

My life is opening up in more extraordinary ways than I could have imagined but I'm ready for even more.

I've come to know the earth medicine that soothes my soul and I allow this magic to work its way into the parts of me that still ache and carry the tears of all that is unjust and raw as I gently come home to my true divine self.

Here I find my power to rise in love and still carry the stories that must be told to heal, unify and evolve the collective consciousness.

A Blessing for Clarity

I am in deep resonance with who I'm becoming.

I invest my energy into those experiences and people who light up my world and reward me in immeasurable ways.

My command of my own personal power is reaching new heights.

I see limitless opportunities and move boldly towards the life that waits patiently for me to value myself enough to align with it.

I navigate each and every twist and turn, rising over challenges and unearthing even more strength and confidence on my way.

I see myself fully realising my potential and in a beautiful state of readiness to receive more for myself.

I love who I am, I love who I'm becoming, I love the life I'm living and I get to decide what's next.

Everything is changing for the better.

I find the frequency of love in everything that I say and do today.

I embody my truth without the need for validation.

I own every part of my beautiful, complicated and chaotic life. It's the perfect place to welcome where my soul is guiding me next.

The only place I need to be right now is present with myself.

A Blessing for Heart Healing

May you find ways to dance lightly between the highs and the lows.

May you seek new inspiration that takes you beyond where you thought possible.

May you find new appreciation in those things that continue to shine for you.

May you find potential wrapped inside what you thought had been lost.

May you find truth when you speak yours.

May you hear the words you have been longing for.

May you be open to find connections that elevate and encourage you.

May you seek comfort as the changing energies challenge you and the earth holds you.

May destiny deliver what your soul needs to feel and your heart needs to heal.

A Blessing for Starseeds

May you invite in the light to illuminate the way forward and soothe your soul in the acceptance of where you find yourself in this transition.

May you find grace and respect in all that you have experienced, whilst continuing to open your heart to the potential that now emanates from your evolved and awakened soul.

May you shed the layers that weigh heavy with doubt.

May you honour yourself by finding the courage to be who you want to be and give full and divine permission to move forward with unwavering hope and unshakeable belief in your ability to rise.

May you find peace if you have trouble in your soul.

May you wake up to the sacred flame of your own sensitive and vibrant spirit.

May you trust again where your soul has splintered and may you find the pieces create an even more beautiful vision as you heal and they fuse with new deeper wisdom.

May you move effortlessly into this new cycle that whispers your name, calling you to be more, to seek more, to receive more.

May you find yourself in the wild and realize that it was always home.

May you feel whole and may you find love, unity and purpose.

May you be willing to be misunderstood as you make changes that better serve your soul.

May you receive the blessings of calmness, clarity and wisdom to make choices that bring you joy.

May you dare to dream bigger, demand more and question everything so as to discover what you now need to feel aligned in your pathway of purpose.

May you see yourself as worthy, capable and deserving of what you desire and ready to receive better for yourself.

May you know your true self and the journey you've taken to reach this moment.

A Blessing for Calm

I am a symphony of changeable energies and I don't need to alter this about myself.

Today I will realise that it takes people different times to adjust to the energy shifts of awakening and I will activate greater tolerance and forgiveness towards myself for being triggered by their words and their projections.

I will surround myself in healing white light and affirm I am okay exactly where I am, even when things don't feel as aligned as I hoped they would be.

I will not move into sabotaging or panic-based thoughts, rather I will step by step – observe, release, review and allow myself to come back into my own energy field. This is where my answers lay waiting to strengthen and clarify things for me.

I will soothe my soul by listening to what my higher self wants me to know is certain for me, and I will trust this wisdom as I seek to experience the wholeness that is being illuminated within me.

I will receive a wave of calm moving through me at some point today that will feel heaven-sent. I will notice it and thank the angels who've wrapped me in their love.

A Blessing for Harmony

May you awaken on peaceful shores.

May you feel nourished and cleansed and in a beautiful state of awakened flow.

May you find peace within the crystal waters of your soul.

May you rise on waves of light that carry you where your heart belongs.

May your senses be flooded with faith and fortitude.

May the words you hear be blessed with love.

May the truth you speak be said with courage.

May the release you allow be wrapped in grace.

May your soul family be all that you seek so that you may express all that you are.

May your legacy spill forth from a place of peace to pave your path with new vibrations of joy.

May the healing you search for emerge from the strength of your spirit.

May you return home to yourself lovingly endlessly and consciously.

A Blessing for Gratitude

May gratitude dissolve the anger in your thoughts.

May it soothe the rejection in your heart.

May it relieve the burdens that weigh heavy on your mind.

May it comfort you in the loss.

May it guide you out of the darkness.

May it encourage you with dreams that burn brightly in your soul.

May it end the turmoil of not being enough.

May it highlight the recognition of how far you've come.

May it direct you inwards to the light of your potential and the destiny of your journey, still unfolding, still becoming, still growing into a healing garden of beauty, wisdom and love.

Affirmations for joy

I think new thoughts that are brighter, bolder and chase the horizon of possibility as I seek more for myself in the adventure of life. I am shaping new beliefs with every step I take to carve original pathways in unchartered lands of mystery and magic. Energy is transforming before my eyes and I witness the evolution with certainty that I'm in the right place at the right time. I accept my worthiness to receive the blessings that are flowing into the spaces I've created to nurture them. I've never been more ready to allow joy into my path. Fate is about to connect me to extraordinary new experiences and my heart is already expanding to receive them.

I feel deeply into the quiet space that whispers secrets of where I am rising like the Phoenix and transforming my life into something epic and empowered. I merge with those souls who sing my song and together we become more. This moment is beautiful and I let myself fall into its magical waters. It breathes life back into all that is ready to come alive and I feel complete.

I will recognise the true light of my soul and embrace where I see this mirrored in those I connect with as I blossom in the richness of loving and respecting myself more day by day. I thrive when I embrace the best of myself. So many synchronicities fall into my journey as I realise what's been waiting patiently for me all along. Peace rises up like a chorus of angels and I let it flood my senses as I meet the abundance of love that's destined to envelop me from this day forth.

Activate your Heart Energy

Take the next 3 minutes to soothe your soul.

For the first 60 seconds,

Tell yourself all the ways you are proud of yourself for dealing with what you've got going on in your pathways at this time.

Invite white light to flood the space around you.

For the next 60 seconds,

Focus on one person and remind yourself of all the reasons you love and appreciate them.

Send white light to them.

For the final 60 seconds,

Repeat the statement "*my body feels at peace when*"...

Now speak all the things that make you feel calm in your physical body and draw white light around you.

Give yourself permission to stay in the vibration of calm today.

Activate the Sun

Today you are the Sun, your light is radiant and warm, and it charges your physical energy continuously.

You feel energised, vital and alive.

Draining people and situations do not affect you as you hold your power and draw strength from the sacred light that emanates from within you.

This golden energy protects you, inspires you and fills your heart with love and positive expectations.

Feel this charge moving through your light body and igniting your Solar Plexus.

Lower vibrations cannot harm you or disconnect you from your source.

You are vibrating higher.

You are the light.

You stand in the light.

You are protected by the light.

Activate your Visions

Activate your destiny.

Activate your highest timelines for growth.

Activate your desire for peace.

Activate deeper balance and breath.

Activate dreams and embody their energy.

Activate sacred rest and rejuvenation.

Activate higher spiritual truth.

Activate a new willingness for trust.

Activate a river of divine abundance.

Activate a stream of consciousness to illuminate the way.

Activate the wisdom and the wonder.

Activate divine devotion to your spiritual heart and rise in love.

Activate the union of higher conscious connections.

Activate a readiness to expand beyond your current perceptions of reality to witness the miracles waiting for you.

You've Changed

You've changed...

Your soul has a plan in this lifetime. Each year it offers you a map through the cosmos. You return many times over to the same stars, and the same oceans, traversing the familiar mountain ranges and trekking over the churned-up soil you have encountered repeatedly through the changing seasons.

Meeting yourself over and over again until you find the resonance of your true self, each visit unearthing more trust and revealing more light as you dance with the divine.

Every connection with another soul acts as a catalyst for change and growth, to heal old wounds, and to call back your energy so that you become your own healing medicine, creating alchemy as you transform into a closer expression of the loving vibrational being that you are.

A complex route has been walked, of that, there is no doubt, yet no matter how many times you lost yourself, the story reset from where you left it and endlessly called you forward.

Pause in this moment to see how you've changed. It's not only been about finding out who you are, it's been about remembering who you've always been.

Your heart has expanded through the love and the loss. Through the inspiration and the richness that has shown itself to you as you survived the most colourful mosaic pathway that has been your life so far.

Hold your head up sweet soul.

You've changed and it's a beautiful thing.

Inhale Light to Exhale Peace

In a moment of respite, the fusing of energies around you creates a rainbow archway to feel your way through. Each colourful hue cleanses your soul as you pass beneath it. A waterfall of light cascades to shower you with renewed hope and beautiful visions as you stand in this moment in between worlds. You are not lost here you're simply standing in the exhale and enlightened by the experience. Send this healing to those who need to feel the strength of your steady heartbeat.

Whispering trees ask you to slow down, to remind yourself where you are, to connect with your deepest truth. See the next step before you, imagine your feet falling on soft ground and the cool breeze revitalizing your tired eyes. Watch every detail move into place and experience the coalescing of all that you desire. Take the step over and over and over again until it feels so familiar you wonder if it's already happened and this just feels like déjà vu.

Your power lies not in the reaction to the forces swirling around you, but in the strength of your vision. The trust in your higher self and the ability to open to your unique soul journey.

This is a soul revolution. A reignition, a renewal, and a reminder from the ancient ones that walk by your side and invite you to see beyond the surface of things and to the truth that shines beneath.

Let the healing waters cleanse you and release your grip on what's already done. Watch where the rivers flow and be guided by them as they carve their way through troubled lands, making way for new ideas and inspirations to emerge that will soothe your anxious mind and show you where to find yourself again.

Allow yourself to be swept up in the flow of new beginnings and find faith in the promise of a fresh start. Dare to dream with more vibrancy, proclaiming every detail to yourself and be unafraid to challenge and change what no longer feels true for you.

Although this is bigger than you, it will always begin with you.

Inhale your light and exhale your peace.

This is the Way. This is the Work

Are you ready to lean in?

Even when it doesn't feel familiar, even when it challenges you to find more tolerance and forgiveness as the fickle tides of your emotions want to carry you deeper into the void.

Are you ready to trust again?

To feel the desires that are wildly coursing through your veins and express them to the world without fear as you stand in your divine power. To make no apology for what it takes to honour your self-preservation, ready to release the energy of anything that cannot accept the magic and depth of your illuminated soul.

Have you found acceptance?

In your sensitivity and your intensity? these are your gifts to the world; do not hide their power and then state you are living a beautiful life. There are mysteries deep as oceans within you, ready to rise up and carve out a new place in this world for a life of connection. A place where soft hearts awaken mighty rivers and the star-filled skies light the way with the maps of stories ready to be remembered and retold.

Can you find your faith?

Knowing that the darkness has held you safe and blinded your sight so that you finally come to remember who you are. Allowing you to exhale forgiveness to those sent to unlock the most wounded parts of your sacred self.

Will you recognise...

How empowered you are right now, forbidding the arrival of any false illusions to deny you of this truth. Awakening to the realisation that you can let go of the exhaustion you attached to the process of regaining your strength and now surrender to this cosmic rebirth.

You wouldn't have made it this far without shattering. It's where the light streams in to allow the expansion to change you.

You have an infinite capacity to rise. To break and become more because of the beautiful light pieces you scatter in the dark so others can find their way.

Your sacred self wants to be connected to more than just your mind right now. Your path doesn't exist just in the words you speak, but in the way you allow yourself to fall deeply into the wisdom of the earth, the cycles of your body, and the infinite expression of intelligence held in the cosmos that you're ethereally bonded to.

This is the way.

This is the work.

You're exceptional, the way you always find your way back to the inner well of strength that gifts you an infinity of reasons to keep going, to start over, to take the pause.

This is the way.

This is the work.

You're so awakened to the moments each day you're about to abandon yourself, but now some things changed. You stop and find the courage in the slow exhale that lets you choose differently.

A choice from a place of peace and higher love. Do you even know the enormity of what that choice just did for you? What that choice just did for all of us? It's so charged with exquisite light you'd see heaven pouring out of you if your eyes could witness the miracle.

This is the way.

This is the work.

Evolving, healing, stumbling, discovering and opening to higher wisdom. You're coded to a blueprint of the future you can't yet see with your physical eyes but your sacred heart knows the way. The map reveals itself more clearly every time you choose to trust yourself.

This is the way.

This is the work.

Take a Breath

How's your faith? is your hope still burning bright? Are your dreams a little weather-beaten but still intact? wherever you are is ok. It's time to find endless patience for all of it. We'll just begin from here, in this brand new moment because all there is, is now.

Start over if you need to, or pick up where you left the unfinished symphony. It's all good, you're right where you're meant to be. Brutally softened by it all but filled with expectation at the promise of possibility that you feel rising within you.

This is your reminder that after every upheaval, disruption and stormy anarchy you are allowed to take some time. To brush away the debris from your thoughts and let your body readjust.

Did you take a breath yet? Ok, now you're ready to see what the horizon looks like. Can you see how the colours changed? There's no room for hindsight, you are where you are and it's the perfect moment to see everything differently, including yourself.

Something new is being birthed right now, it will ask commitment from you, to hold your gaze steady so it can breathe itself into existence, shaped by the light that emanates from within you and the vision you hold steady in your beautiful, chaotic mind.

The patience to persevere is now what's asked of you. Don't worry there is help coming in as you rise up through these clouds. You're so ready to feel lighter, and you will.

They come dressed as optimism, reminding you that you are nowhere near finished, that the best is still becoming, within you, around you, because of you.

They show up as acceptance, understanding that the only way to progress is to be your unique self and to allow everyone else this same gift.

They arrive as generosity, as you discover that the frequency of giving will always raise your vibration letting you see the world from a whole new vantage point, welcoming beautiful moments of realisation at the difference you make in the world.

They present themselves as hope, wrapping silver linings around every single experience that still aches when you gaze towards it. And they whisper to you that there is so much more to you.

They charge in with resourcefulness bringing brand new possibilities that offer you stepping stones to rise up from every experience that has tested you.

Together they beat the slow and steady drums of harmony and you will feel their deep melodic rhythm move you back into a place of flow where your soul rests, poised to embrace the love that is always there for you.

Acts of Grace

You keep turning back but the path no longer exists. How you connect to yourself is changing, and with it the direction you're moving in.

Deep wisdom emerging from your journey now directs you to recognise who you are beneath the stories that are tired and outdated.

You take care of you with deep respect and acknowledgment of your value, and then they honour you through a more deliberate conscious connection.

You trust you know what's right for you, acting purposefully as you move in greater rhythm to your own powerful inner knowing, and then they respect your energy expression as you walk your true path.

You tend to your own needs, forgiving your resistance and your own self-sabotage to what you truly desire, and then they show up to bring more presence, consistency and nourishment into your life.

You speak kindly and honestly with yourself even when you're moving through the storms, and then you experience deeper more meaningful energetic exchanges with them.

You don't abandon yourself for a quick high or a shortcut to the illusion of a temporary fix and then they stop dismissing your greatness.

You challenge yourself to be better, nurture yourself more and take time to listen to what your soul needs. And then they show up wanting to mirror your dedication to a rich life of meaning, to evolve, grow and blossom into all that you're meant to become.

You become your most loyal champion, recognising how much is still undiscovered in your wells of wisdom and your soulful songs. And then they find mystery and magic in the air you breathe and the presence you hold. Cherishing all that you are without the need to suppress your radiance.

You will always be your greatest love.

Act accordingly.

Divine Knowing

You have to give yourself permission to take up the space you need in this life.

To say no even when it's easier to say yes. And to say yes when it's more comfortable to say no.

To not doubt yourself and the way your body communicates what is best for you.

To trust that sometimes the timing feels like swimming upstream, letting others down, or breaking a belief that's held you protectively for years for something bigger that's calling you.

To love who you love in ways that feel soothing and safe or wild and intoxicating, for your soul is always guiding you to growth through your willingness to experience.

To feel at ease with knowing when it's time to talk and let the words spill forth from your honest heart.

And when it's time to listen and let your presence be a well of nourishment and wisdom for the confessions of those who seek your sanctuary.

And to allow when it's time to nestle into the silence and find peace in the stillness that lives there.

You're unfolding into a galaxy of treasures that have laid quietly sleeping within you, waiting for this season of awakened activation.

This day is laced with precious moments to observe your worthiness. It will mirror back miracles of your being if you let it show you the way.

Place your right hand on your solar plexus and your left hand on your heart. Now breathe in the love you seek, the respect you deserve and the well-being that showers you in light, as you exhale your doubts, your burdens, and the limits you've placed on your readiness to align to the wholeness of your exquisite soul.

Once Upon a Time

Once upon a time, I decided to stop waiting,
I moved my life forward on my own terms.

And the angels of time opened up all the
locked doors.

Once upon a time, the layers of
contradictions in my soul held me back,
but now they're the very things that I
cherish most.

And the angels of love opened up their
wings to hold me.

Once upon a time, I looked at my journey
with an ache that stole my joy, now I see
it through the eyes of a survivor.

And the angels of courage celebrated
with me.

Once upon a time, life offered me
the chance to see everything about
myself differently.

I embraced it with a heart full of gratitude.

And the angels of peace rejoiced with me.

Harmonise your World

Find softness in the things that broke you and pour love and healing into the most tender of places to plant new seeds that will nourish your soul.

You are the alchemist, every choice and decision you make here brings you closer to the future you seek allowing you to make peace with the past.

Fight only for what lifts your spirit, and recommit to what you know must exist to support your peace and harmonise your world.

The power to overcome and succeed against the odds, bringing a depth of wisdom and a legacy of change is energy that is available for you to tap into.

Magnetic conversations are transforming the outlook of your journey. Supporting you to unearth the determination and the will to find a way, to make it through, to have influence and accountability over the outcomes as you stand purposefully and meaningfully in the direction of your dreams.

It's a season of magic, deep and thought-provoking in its ability to awaken something within you as you bring the light of the Sun to the shadows of your doubt.

May you empower yourself to look in the direction of where doors are opening for you and become the catalyst for the beauty of your own metamorphosis.

You are making steady and consistent progress toward necessary change and positive transformation.

Some kind of wonderful will fall into place for you as you open to lovingly receive it.

You have time because your peace is your priority.

Prioritise your Peace

There will be all sorts of situations and energies that try to disconnect you from yourself.

Prioritise your peace.

There will be conversations that trigger or confuse you.

Prioritise your peace.

People will choose to hear or receive from you only that which they are energetically aligned. Their response does not define you, nor should it give you cause to feel frustrated, unworthy, anxious, disappointed, or misunderstood.

Prioritise your peace.

Your energy levels may fluctuate wildly bringing to the surface doubt, exhaustion, overwhelm or fear. Breathe, know that you will find your sacred rhythm again, and trust these emotions are valuable teachers, here to help you evolve faster than ever before.

Prioritise your peace.

Energy doesn't lie, so be mindful and consciously awakened to what you're bringing to every encounter, the thoughts you're thinking, the words you're expressing and the way you depart every situation.

What energy legacy did you leave?

That's the vibe you'll be meeting again before long. Stay kind. Stay loving. Stay tolerant.

Prioritise your peace.

Keep seeking the antidote to what disrupts your peace, not focusing on the cause of it.

There will be moments you doubt yourself and try to go against your intuition and lessen all that you are.

Don't.

Trust in your path.

There will be beautiful moments that you might struggle to celebrate or enjoy for a myriad of different reasons.

Embrace them fully without guilt. They are a gift just for you.

There will be unexpected emotions that surface and blindside you. Accept them without resistance and honour your need to process them in your own time and in your own way.

Trust in your path.

There will be two responses available to you at any given moment. One that is kind and from a place of love and one that is disconnected and from a place of the wound.

Don't judge yourself for the choices you make as each will teach you something of value.

Trust in your path.

Moving Forward

Now is when you must fiercely grasp the parts of your life that no longer make sense, shapeshifting them into something that awakens you.

Life happens in those moments of discomfort and crisis where the urgency to change overrides the desire to self-abandon and stay stuck.

Every moment delivers a choice to come home to yourself. Stand in your strength and soften into the rising certainty that emerges when you know what's right for you.

The way forward might look very different than what you'd anticipated, so take some time to look at this from a place of non-judgement and unearth what the gain for you could be.

Don't rush into anything you may later feel was never right for you. Trust in your first gut reaction.

You can navigate any conflict or challenge beautifully right now when you are led by your inner guidance. There is no need to declare your position or justify your feelings if that isn't sitting right with you at this moment, just quietly trust your own path and maintain an open and receptive state so you can follow the flow and find your way forward.

Don't allow comparison to creep in, the thought that you need to be more assertive, more vocal, and more available is just an illusion. Your unique gifts of thoughtful and considered wisdom and understanding are what will bring you to the destination that you're seeking.

There is no weakness in following your heart. It's more powerful energy than any external guidance you will receive, but you're being asked to be discerning and respectful of what you've just learned about yourself and grow from the experiences.

A defensive or hostile stance will not deliver you the justice, emotional connection, or fulfilment you are seeking right now, being true to your own compassionate nature and coming from a place of inner balance is the answer.

Don't seek validation for your actions, but trust that you will see the impact of your energy and you will benefit in greater ways than you can see and even than you are asking for right now as things move in divine time. Your guides have your back right now let them bring in cosmic detours for your highest good.

There are no sentences that should begin with "Just".

I'm "just checking, I'm Just asking, I'm just making sure...they all start with an apology which is not yours to make. Rise up and speak your truth.

There are no wrong roads to take, each one is beautifully crafted by you and your energy, and each challenge is the illumination from inside for you to heal something that is holding you back. It's time to shift your perspective on everything and then feel the sense of freedom and liberation that brings you.

Higher Purpose

It's a time to dream big feel and heal as you witness the energy coalesce in your pathways and introduce you to a glimpse of your future that will feel surreal and fated.

The alignment to a higher purpose is unearthed, dissolving limitations and preparing you for brave acts of love and compassion that bring you closer to your divine connection.

New energy that awakens a movement and reveals new discoveries that change perceptions and permanently alter outdated beliefs is unfolding.

The spiritual journey is embraced with deeper understanding and reverence and new teachers, leaders, and guides emerge ready to facilitate the next level of consciousness and growth.

In this cosmic conversation, a wave of new artistic and creative influences is born. Healing and compassion flow into the shadows and casts light to transmute the density of what tries to hold back the collective from evolving toward unity consciousness.

Expansion and rapid growth collapse your understanding of timelines as old wisdom surfaces to join new downloads and blessings are carried on oceans of possibility.

It's a beguiling exchange in the currents of time where new mythology is born and profound realisations are felt. If you're looking for the moments where magic is born then look no further. Summon it towards you through your acceptance of the greater divine order and step through this portal and it will forever change your understanding of yourself and what exists beyond the veil.

Work with this alchemical blend of spellbinding proportions as you stand in the intersection of past and future and let yourself be inextricably pulled higher in purpose, presence and peace.

Find forgiveness and seek answers that stretch your mind and facilitate your growth. Look for spiritual keys that shine with honesty and integrity and that feel like home even when they crack open your mind in extraordinary new ways.

Don't let the fantasy and illusion carry you out to sea. The dissolving haze can overwhelm and tether you addictively to situations that blow up quickly and consume your energy.

Ride high on the awakened agenda of exquisite bountiful blessings. New visions and gifts are sailing towards you, greet them with a readiness to evolve and be a better human so you may express the unconditional and loving source of your soul's light.

Elemental Dance

I hope you don't take things personally today. Everyone has their own kind of metamorphosis unfolding and some days it's a little messy for us all.

I hope you grasp the enormity of consciously choosing a better thought and another and another.

I hope you remember why you started.

I hope you ask for help and then actually allow yourself to receive it.

I hope you acknowledge the significance of letting the emotion wash over you without feeling "less than" because of it.

I hope you accept the phase you're in isn't the entirety of what you're capable of, what you're going to experience and the beauty that's still destined for you.

I hope you'll choose not to tolerate the projection, but still find compassion for those who've lost their way.

I hope you go seeking today all of the wildflowers that teach you how to grow anywhere that offers you the richness of good earth, the warmth of sunlight, and the freedom to be you.

I hope you choose to keep shape-shifting like the clouds, always forming new expressions of energy as you adapt to the elemental dance of change that surrounds you, but never defines you.

Your North Star

Time to lighten up on yourself.

Time to come home to yourself.

Little by little.

Thought by thought.

Breath by breath.

There is a new soul song blossoming for you here, so be here and all in.

You may feel you want to be somewhere you're not perhaps with someone different or doing something else. Focus on this can bring resistance to your energy.

You are not going to miss out, mess up or lose anything that is already divinely yours.

It's very important that you listen carefully right now. To yourself and the thoughts you think, to the words being said to you in response to your vibrational expression. To conversations you observe and information you tune into on the physical and spiritual planes. It will give you a direct map of what is coming next. The themes you will be working on and how you can more easily make peace with situations knowing their time to change and transform your life is here.

Your thoughts are literally being rewired. One by one you will release limiting beliefs and as you confront and revisit them you will step more deeply into a state of surrender, peace and transcendence.

Each belief represents a false truth that you must shatter so that you can free yourself and walk forwards boldly, filled with renewed self-belief about what's next for you.

You will come to meet your new truths and as you do you will find compassion for yourself and others in their revelation. Some may surprise you; some may challenge you, but all will serve you in all the ways that you need them to.

This takes bravery and you are ready.

This takes courage and you have it.

This takes strength and you've built it.

You have all that you need to meet the present moment and to be fully here with its blessings as it transforms you.

There is nothing to fear, in fact, you are willingly seeking to face these things so you can give yourself permission to be more, to have greater depth, meaning and fulfilment in your life.

Sometimes we invite stress because it sharpens our focus on what is out of alignment. Finding presence will help loosen the binds that tie you.

There is a solution to a situation you feel blocked in. It requires patience, awareness and openness. When you listen you will receive what you need to see from a future perspective with the knowing that you do make it, that it does change that you can shift this energy.

This time invites in more play, more lightness more tenderness, but you must open your eyes to it sweet soul. Don't bury yourself in the "what if" live each breath fully and you will bring magic into things you felt were not going anywhere.

This is a powerful time of expansion; you have to go with this levelling up. It's ok to feel uncertain or doubtful but keep honouring the changes so you don't stay stuck. A whole kingdom of dreams is making its way to the surface for you.

You are releasing old beliefs to allow divine timing to deliver the most beautiful destiny. All things meant for you are showing up in the most surprising and unexpected ways and you embrace them fully as you vibrate higher.

Open to Trust

Knowing that you want to change and creating time, space and intention to allow this growth, is supported beautifully as you open to greater self-trust.

You have so much influence over what comes next for you. The timing couldn't be more perfect to welcome the energy of change in your life. Let go of the illusion that you have no options right now.

You have comfort zones, projected fear from others, and the momentum of old energy cycles that have come to a point of closure. None of which can dictate this week if you choose to experience something more for yourself.

Take this time to say something new to yourself about yourself. You're wildly more capable than you've ever been. And the clouds that may have lingered over your remembrance of this truth, never took away the strength of the sun's rays to support you blossoming into your brilliance.

Observe how you increasingly move away more easily from what drains, disappoints and dares to define you as not enough.

You're radiating a new level of inner confidence, even if you haven't yet road tested what that feels like, let the acknowledgment of what you've navigated in your journey give you the cosmic boost and recognition of how evolved you're becoming in your own journey.

Your power is a quiet certainty of self. Act intentionally and honour this awareness as you invite in extraordinary discoveries about how you've held yourself back, and then make decisions about how you are moving beyond this chapter to something entirely created by the fusion of your own dreams, self-actualisation, greatness and readiness to receive.

Layers of Light

As you sit in a place of contemplation about your many layers, the seemingly opposing aspects of who you are, and the split desires that leave you ruminating at what energy you are supposed to align with, a soul song of truth emerges.

You may find yourself reflective of the different masks you choose to wear to the world. How you shift and move from one role to another and how easy or tiresome that is becoming. Perhaps of late, it has felt a little weary, leaving you restless even. Trying to fit in only serves at times to make you feel more alone or out of place.

With an increasing awareness that feels there must be more to life, you are being coaxed out of your normal routine. And to accept that you are not meant to dampen down any part of yourself.

You can play many characters within your life as long as each one allows you to express yourself and nourishes an aspect of the inner you. Any role that doesn't fit with these intentions will start to feel uncomfortable and false, encouraging you to assess and take a new approach to how you want to show up and how you want to be seen.

In the duality that resides within, you are a soul that can be in motion and yet find stillness. You can share your voice and express your love, but find quiet contemplation and connection within.

You are meant to be a series of contradictions so don't fight the need to be many things all at once. When you follow a path that feels right for you, your energy lights up everything and everyone around you.

Sometimes you also need to experience the crashing waves, the noise that seems to drown out all other signs. Although at times it may feel like it's overwhelming and silencing your inner call, it is serving a purpose and helping you to marry together the many aspects of yourself in a deeper acceptance, knowing the truth that there will perpetually be light and shade that exists for you on your path and in these moments, you are safe and all is well.

Pay close attention to the nourishment you are giving yourself. Where people, events and situations disrupt you don't be afraid to step away and consider who you want to be in this moment.

Remember purpose and presence will be your light through any clouds that surface and temporarily block your vision.

Don't be defined or confined by anyone or anything.

Take charge, take flight and find your light.

Be all in

Because you have so many layers and they speak in a chorus of conflicting energies and emotions to your head and your heart, and that's okay, and you're okay.

When you're guided to do things from your inner wisdom, acting with integrity and honouring your unique soul path...

Sometimes others won't understand your choices. Be all in for your decisions and stand by them regardless.

Sometimes asserting necessary boundaries means others will judge and feel let down by you. Be all in for what creates balance in your life regardless.

Sometimes your coping mechanisms for healing will deeply trigger and cause chaos for those around you. Be all in for your path to recovery and health regardless.

The domino effect of your actions will always impact people and situations in your life, often splitting your energy and causing doubt to be cast over your own intuitive knowing because of the reactionary vibrations that are activated around you.

Your commitment to self must be a seeker of peace in the uncomfortable, challenging space that is created when not everyone aligns, supports or respects you during your growth.

As you honour this process for yourself, you will find more acceptance in how others choose to walk their path, releasing yourself from any discomfort of your own expectations not being met by them, but wholly honouring your needs, wants and desires without compromise.

Spiritual Assignment

I spent my whole life looking for a way in to feel part of this world. I knocked on so many doors, accepted so many labels, and tried out so many versions of myself, but none of them ever felt like home.

There's been the ache of loneliness inside of me my whole life that no relationship, connection or experience could ever fully quiet.

I've questioned and I've contemplated. I've meditated and healed. I've reflected on all of the ways I was led by my guides so that I may meet this part of myself and come to terms with her.

Doing the inner work soothes the yearning and I alchemise the ache daily, but she's never far beneath the surface of my thoughts. Being in this world but never feeling a part of it, I've come to accept, doesn't mean I won't still welcome deep joy, fulfil burning desires and be grateful for the experiences that help me to love, grow, inspire and guide.

We heal and then we teach.

It's a lifelong journey where there are more questions than answers.

When your soul is restless and the sacred loneliness is calling, there's a special spiritual assignment you've accepted in this lifetime.

It's brave and beautiful and will let you see and feel things so richly that the ways in which you allow it to crack you open help the world to heal and the Universe to become more.

Love this part of yourself, it's sacred and reminds you that there is so much more held in our galaxy that you've been a part of and are still connected to.

It all begins with me.
I am the love that I desire.
I am the safe harbour that I need.
I am the wholeness that I seek.
In discovering myself I find peace.
Where I let the light flow,
I transcend the patterns that get tangled in my soul.
My Life.
My Soul.
My Vision.
All that I am is blessed with all that is.
New adventures await and so I take a long slow exhale,
I'm ready for this.

Honour your Journey

Time to honour your journey...

With respect for how you showed up on the days that unravelled you.

The triggers that challenged you and the moments that crushed you.

With appreciation for the time spent with the people who felt like home.

For the nature and animals that soothed you and the peace that held you.

With recognition for the progress you've made.

At times leaping and leveling up in ways you'd never expected, but also for the days when you held yourself through the fear and anxiety, the overwhelm and the exhaustion.

With relief that you started to listen more openly to the body that was teaching you what needed to change.

To the thoughts that were controlling you and needed to evolve.

To the emotions that were revealing to you what was ready to be healed.

With love for the life you're creating for yourself so happiness can thrive, and the challenging decisions you made to honour this sacred heart commitment.

With acknowledgement for what you learned, what you lost, and how it changed you.

With humility to what you've witnessed and the stories you've held space for. The progress you made as you moved on, moved through and moved up.

For the light inside that never stopped endlessly guiding you home to yourself.

With humour for the craziness of it all and the laughter that broke the silence and flooded light into the heaviness.

With acceptance of the miracles, so many beautiful tiny heart-filled blessings that brought richness and meaning and connection and joy.

With the energies that harmonised you to a new frequency to meet yourself with fresh eyes and humility to bow to the greatness of the Earth's gifts.

How it's changed you this assortment of mutable days and extraordinary moments all laced together with hope and love and endless courage.

I'm proud of you.

You met each moment with all that you had to give.

And it was enough.

@romy.wyser

@lifesoulvision

@romywyser

@romywyser

romywyser.com

About the Author

Romy Wyser is a Spiritual Leader, a renowned Professional Intuitive, Author and Tarot Reader.

Romy guides and inspires people all over the world with her uniquely channeled insights and soulful wisdom to support spiritual growth and self-awareness.

Romy continues to nurture and hold a safe and elevated vibrational space to connect, reflect and come back into harmony with your mind, body and soul.

Romy calls Scotland home where she enjoys a peaceful life in the country with her two Golden Retrievers, Shiya and Angel. Here she enjoys the blessings of nature that keep her grounded and soothe her soul whilst she creates, mentors, and writes with passion and dedication to her spiritual path.

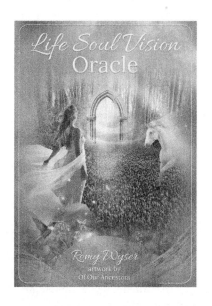

ROMY WYSER

Printed in Great Britain
by Amazon

22173977R00106